TABLE OF CONTENTS

CW00461068

DISCOVER SCOTLAND CULTURE, SPORTS, HISTORY, CUISINE, LANDMARKS, PEOPLE, TRADITIONS AND MANY MORE FOR KIDS

....

....

ABOUT SCOTLAND

Part of the United Kingdom.

Capital city – Edinburgh.

Three official languages: English, Scots, and Scottish Gaelic.

Population – 5.4 Million

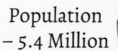

Country has rich history and lot of mythological stories, including the Loch Ness Monster.

National Day - St. Andrew's Day, - November 30th.

National animal – unicorn.

Country has its own legal system separate from England and Wales.

Scottish children like wear kilts on special occasions.

Scottish inventions - telephone and the television.

GEOGRAPHY

Total 790 islands but 130 are inhabited.

Highest point is Ben Nevis.

Surround by the Atlantic Ocean, North Sea, Irish Sea, and the English Channel.

Many deep lakes called - 'lochs'.

Famous lake called Loch Ness - people say a monster lives.

Longest river - River Tay.

Largest national park in UK - the Cairngorms.

The country landscape for its rugged beauty and green glens

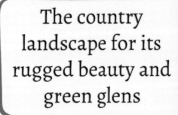

NATIONAL SYMBOLS

National emblem – thistle.

Flag is blue with a white cross – called as Saltire.

Tartan – Pattern seen on kilts it's known as clan heritage.

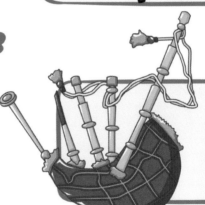

Traditional musical instrument Bagpipes.

Lion rampant is a royal symbol.

Haggis - national symbol of food.

Country banknotes unique designs from the rest of the UK.

National tree – Oak Tree.

Globally recognized product whisky.

Crown of Scotland is a national symbol found in Edinburgh Castle.

WEATHER

The climate can change many times in a day

In highlands particularly in winter times very cold, with snow and ice.

May be - "Four seasons in a day".

Summer are mild not too hot.

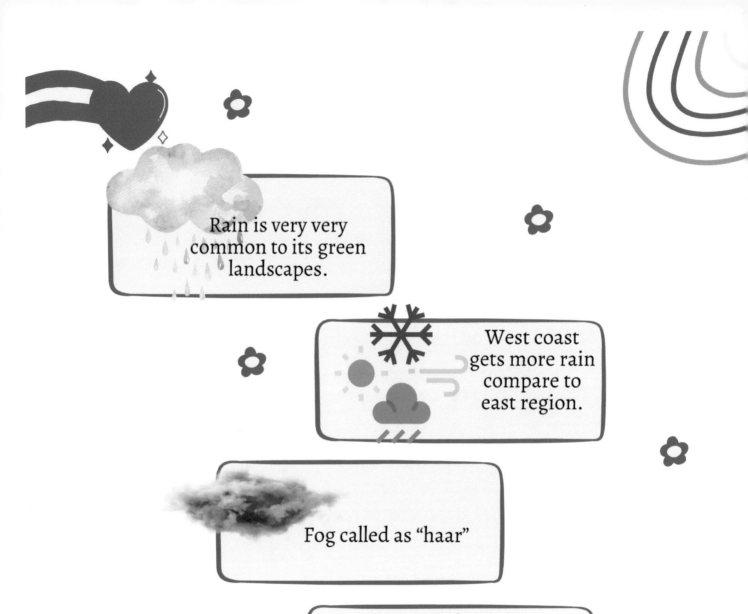

Rain is very very common to its green landscapes.

West coast gets more rain compare to east region.

Fog called as "haar"

From north to west experience strong winds. The sunniest regions – northern highlands because it's high altitude.

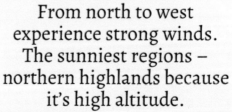

CONSTITUTION

Country has its own parliament for Scottish issues.

It was established in 1999 after a referendum.

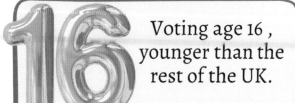

It give make decision on education, health, and justice.

Voting age 16, younger than the rest of the UK.

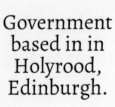
Government based in in Holyrood, Edinburgh.

United Kingdom's Parliament in London dealing certain areas like defense and foreign affairs.

Scottish law dealing both civil and common law.

NATIVE ANIMALS

Scottish wildcat - rarest animals in the world.

Puffins - colourful beaks.

Red deer - largest land mammal.

Golden Eagle - famous birds of prey.

Highland Cow - long hair and horns.

Atlantic salmon.

Red squirrels.

Orkney vole - found only in Orkney.

Scottish seal.

Pine Marten - small, rare, and protected predator.

NATIVE PLANTS

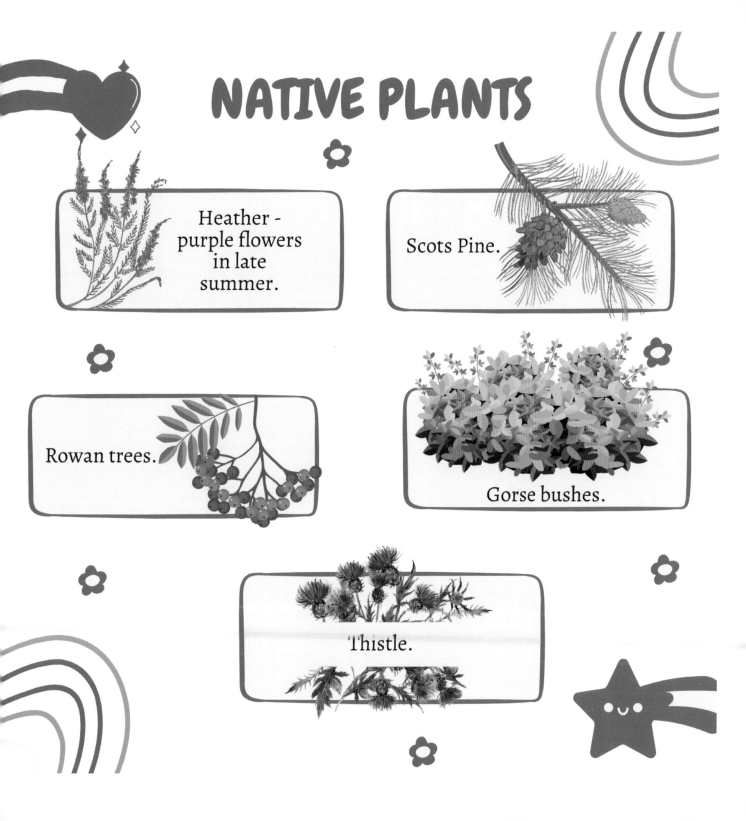

Heather - purple flowers in late summer.

Scots Pine.

Rowan trees.

Gorse bushes.

Thistle.

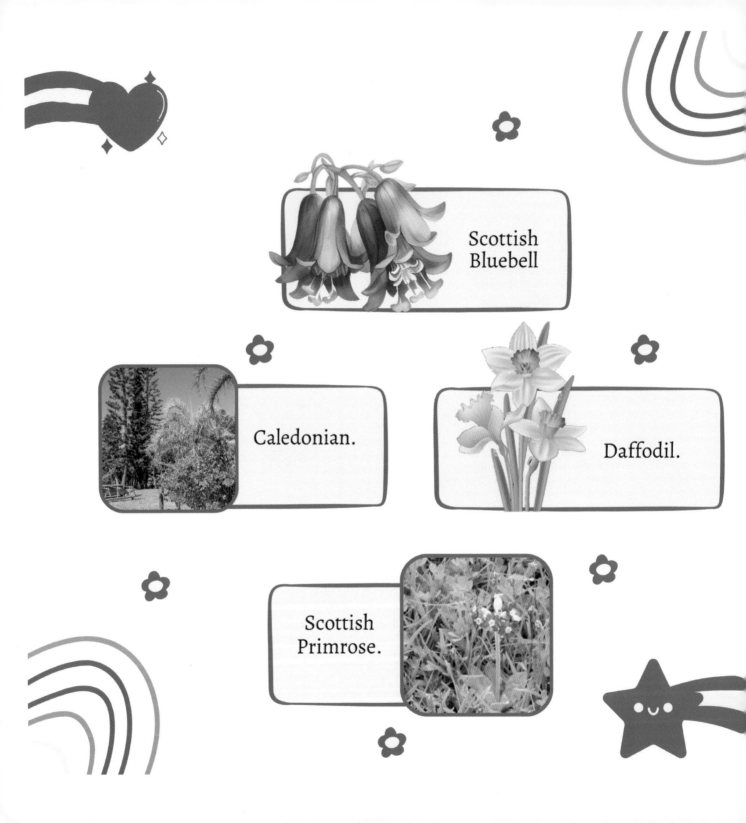

Scottish Bluebell

Caledonian.

Daffodil.

Scottish Primrose.

FAMOUS PEOPLE

Alexander Graham Bell - inventor of the telephone.

Sir Walter Scott – writer.

Andrew Carnegie - industrialist and philanthropist.

Mary-Queen of Scots.

David Hume-philosopher and historian.

Sean Connery- actor playing James Bond.

Robert Burns- poet- his birthday is celebrated as Burns Night.

Adam Smith – economist - author of "The Wealth of Nations."

Alexander Fleming discovered penicillin.

Annie Lennox- award-winning musician.

LANDMARKS & ARCHITECTURE

Edinburgh Castle.

Forth Bridge - Firth of Forth and a UNESCO World Heritage Site.

Stirling Castle.

Kelpies - two 30-meter-high horse-head.

Skara Brae - best-preserved Stone Age villages in Europe.

Glasgow School of Art.

Falkirk Wheel-rotating boat lift.

Royal Mile is a historic street.

Holyrood Palace - residence of the Queen.

Wallace Monument.

CULTURE AND CUISINE

Kilts and tartans – traditional dress.

Bagpipes – traditional instrument

Haggis – traditional dish made from sheep's offal and oatmeal.

Whisky - single malt Scotch.

During Christmas and Hogmanay shortbread is a buttery cookie is popular.

Ceilidh – social gathering with folk music and dancing.

Porridge – traditional breakfast.

Clan gatherings and games.

FESTIVALS AND CELEBRATIONS

Hogmanay - Scottish New Year celebration.

Edinburgh Festival Fringe – largest festival in the world.

Burns Night – January 25th.

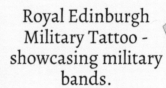

Royal Edinburgh Military Tattoo - showcasing military bands.

Up Helly Aa - Viking fire festival.

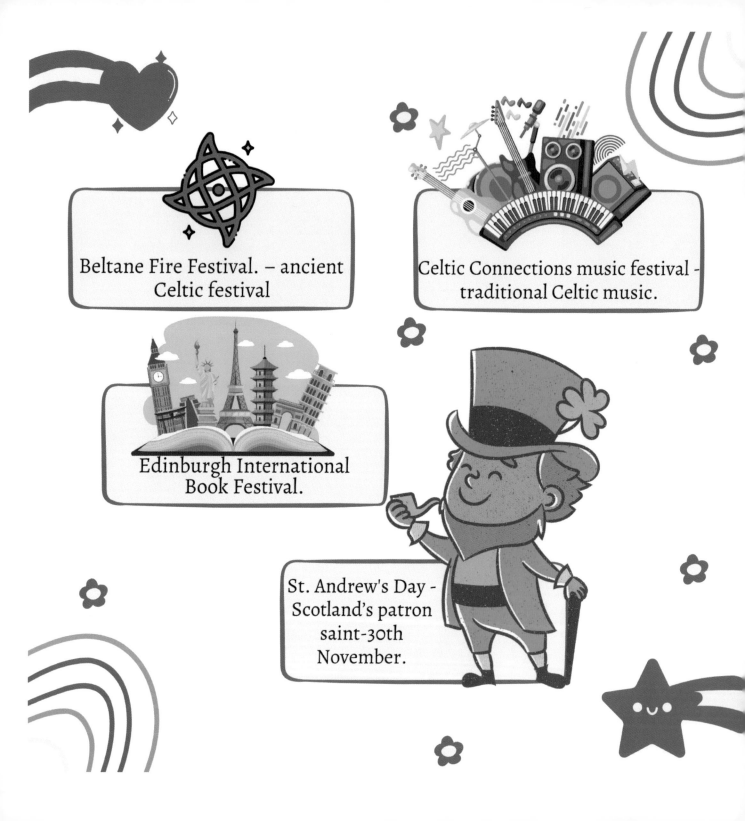

Beltane Fire Festival. – ancient Celtic festival

Celtic Connections music festival - traditional Celtic music.

Edinburgh International Book Festival.

St. Andrew's Day - Scotland's patron saint-30th November.

SPORTS

Golf invented
in Scotland –
"Home of golf"
- St. Andrews.

Rugby.

Soccer - Scottish
Premiership being
the top league.

Shinty,

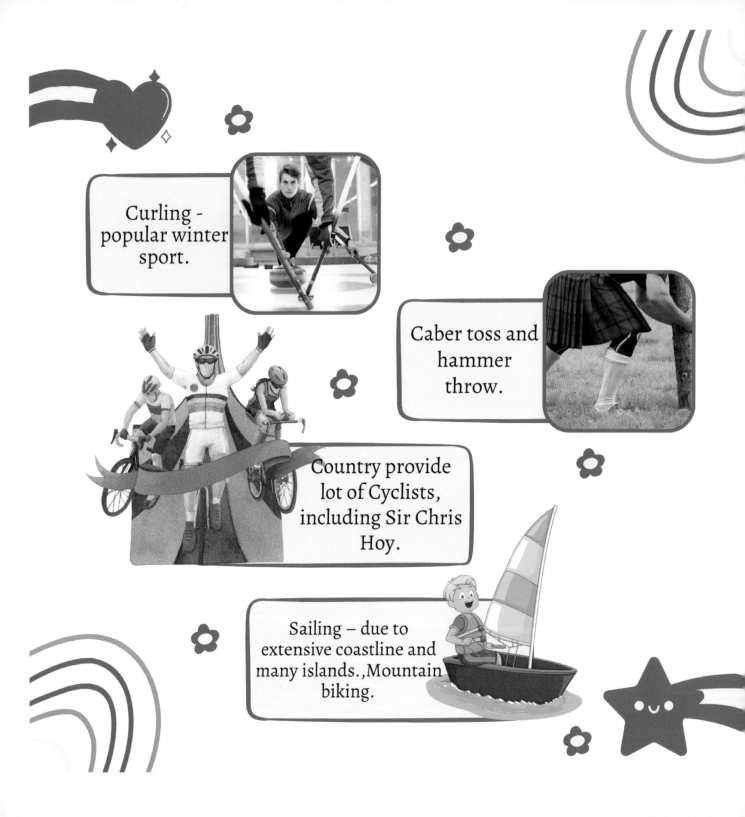

Curling - popular winter sport.

Caber toss and hammer throw.

Country provide lot of Cyclists, including Sir Chris Hoy.

Sailing – due to extensive coastline and many islands.,Mountain biking.

FUN FACTS

Encyclopedia Britannica - first produced.

Raincoat invented by Charles Macintosh.

600 square miles of freshwater lakes.

Shortest scheduled flight it lasts just 1.5 minutes.

In Scotland- First ever official international football match played.

Edinburgh was the first city - own fire brigade.

In Scotland - first cloned mammal, Dolly the sheep.

World's oldest tree- Fortingall Yew- 3,000 years old.

Loch Ness Monster was recorded - 565 AD.

'Maid of the Mist', famous boat tour at Niagara Falls, the name was named after Scottish song.

"Top of the Pops," - longest-running music show in the world- started in Scotland.

John Logie Baird – made the first ever color television broadcast

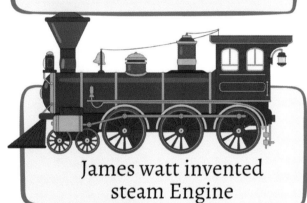

James watt invented steam Engine

College is free in Scotland

"Shinty," game played in Scotland for over 2,000 years, it like hurling.

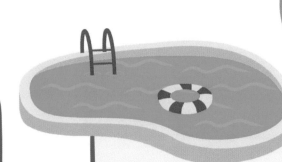

Isle of Skye – having more fairy pools and dramatic landscapes.

January 25th – Country celebrate own Valentine's Day, called St. Dwynwen's Day.

Country has 15 universities University of St Andrews oldest founded in 1413.

Country has own version of Nobel Prize called Carnegie Medal for heroism.

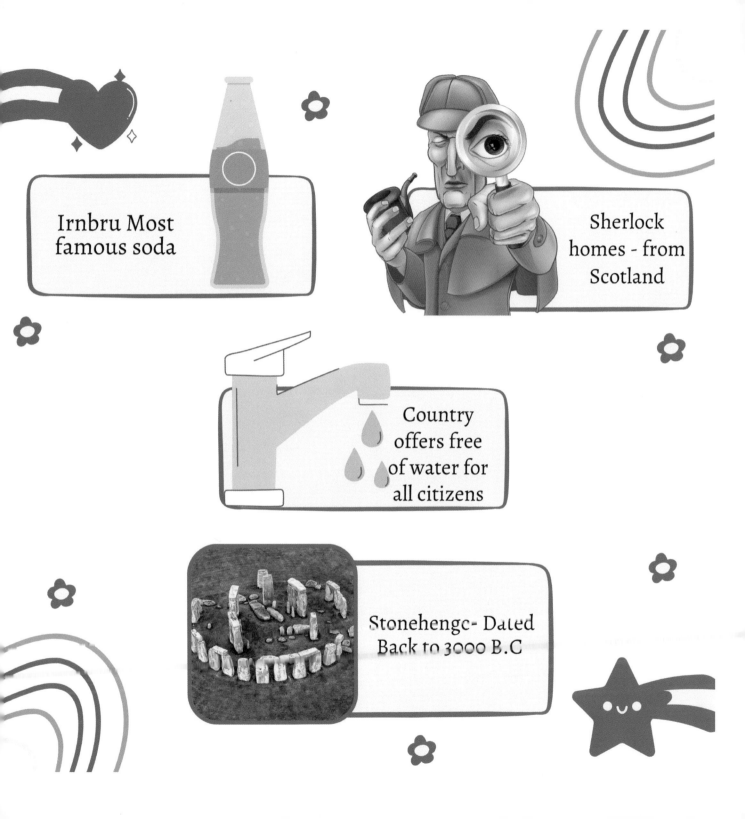

Irnbru Most famous soda

Sherlock homes - from Scotland

Country offers free of water for all citizens

Stonehenge- Dated Back to 3000 B.C

Printed in Great Britain
by Amazon